John Brown was born in Derry in 1961. He studied literature
and history at Bristol University and Edinburgh University. In
the 1980s, he edited *Gown Literary Supplement* in Belfast. He
has recently completed a series of interviews with poets from the
north of Ireland, *In the Chair* (Salmon Press, 2000). He
currently runs a bookshop in Limavady, Co. Derry.

By the same author

Editor
In the Chair:
Interviews with Poets from the North of Ireland

AS THE CROW FLIES

AS THE CROW FLIES

JOHN BROWN

LAGAN PRESS
BELFAST
2003

Acknowledgements are due to the editors of the following magazines in which some of these poems have appeared: Briggestanes, The Chancer, Circa, Fortnight, Gown Literary Supplement, Edinburgh Review, Metre and Skinklin Star.
    '*Morandi*' *was part of an artwork entitled* '*Altar, Alter*' *exhibited in in a group show at the Fenderesky Gallery, Belfast.*
    '*Where Uncle When*' *was published in* A Conversation Piece (Abbey Press, 2002), *an anthology of poetic responses to paintings at the Ulster Museum, Belfast.*

Published by
Lagan Press
138 University Avenue
Belfast BT7 1GZ

ISBN: 1 904652 02 6
Author: Brown, John
Title: As the Crow Flies
2003

Front Cover: Bird (2003) by Tjibbe Hooghiemstra
(reproduced courtesy of the Fenderesky Gallery, Belfast)
Set in Sabon
Printed by Easyprint, Belfast

In memory of Rita Brown

'The birds they sing at break of day
Start again I heard them say.'
—Leonard Cohen

Contents

Eden

Lost by her wisdom,
Faust a beginner
Goes seeking the shining
Light in the tree.
Serpentine wishes.
A fingertip's promise.
Reaching and reaching,
Forever unfree.

Inventory

Five drawers piled up as stairs;
One egg un-donated in the fridge;
Paintbrushs: bald or with stiff hairs;
A formica table dusted down in midges.

Dust motes playing musical chairs.

Lifebuoy soap lathered into a pool of sweat;
Three white squares—once scullery prints;
Two washed-out dockets, either bills or bets;
A Belling cooker over-brimmed in mint.

A shoehorn's suffix. A squeezed tube of lint.

Delivery

Down the fern, hawthorn, gravelled lane,
We are rocking again, where a sleeping dog barks,
Herds the heels of the van to the door.
On breadman day, shelves roared on runners,
A magic display: Paris buns' iced-fine hail;
Snow-rolled coconut balls, pan, plain,
Freckled in fruit; marbled Madeira; Barmbrack;
Vienna—all gifts in a tumbling sun and dogs,
Geese and children run hidden and squawking
Out from a farmwife's frock.
By the van, by the glistering polythene,
A sun-wrapped gift from lanes we've never been.
It'll do, she says, *wi' a drap o' tay*,
As we're pulling away waving,
Leaving iced sugar loaves in the hidden farm
Like a smore of snow
On the red-rimmed frame o' farm machinery.

Where Uncle When

Where uncle when, your hands touch my window sill
Sitting days, there's as much light and shadow at play

As in Tex Ritter's movies. Will you be drawn
From long pockets, silences and loose change

And taken far too slowly to the fair?
Where the magical air takes *whoop* or *look*

No hands, when I'm leaning far out of the saddle
Waving in winds and the splashed crowd melts

In the spume's revolve around
The humping-back horse skewered by golden thread

To the ground. Where uncle when the clown's tent is raised
Still find me running flat out, full of praise

On the yo-yo and swizz of poetry—
Where the grazing horse gilts

And at night or high noon
Shadowless feet don't touch the ground.

Playing

after Tom Waits' 'Georgia Lee'

Do you remember tea towels made us matadors?
You all in ribbons, dressed up as Queen of the Hill:
A flagstone floor; an open door; a sunlit window sill.
Then remember and tell of stars lost in the well
When the bonefire moon stood still.

> *Close your eyes. Count to ten.*
> *Dream like children do again.*
> *Can you find your way across the glen*
> *By foxfire light in the window?*

Do you remember flower-head clocks
Told whether he loved me, or loved me not;
Your dress soaked in patterns of grass freshly cut?
'Til our cup was filled and filled with fire
And the summer house closed up.

> *Close your eyes. Count to ten.*
> *Who will go to find you then?*
> *Will you find your way across the glen*
> *By foxfire light in the window?*

Do you remember playing pea-scoot angels?
All dressed up in lace. A tablecloth for a gypsy shawl.
One-two-three, red lights—then chase.
'Til the world came charging up the hill
And its shadows crossed your face.

> *Close your eyes. Count to ten.*
> *Dream like children do again.*
> *You'll find a way across the glen*
> *By foxfire light in the window.*

The House of the Planter
for Richard Brown

The house of the planter
Is not known by the trees
But by all-night parties.
Nights that are nights from Great Gatsby.
Car headlights ignite circuits
Of red magnolia and leaves.
Village boys paper-bag beer.
And it's said in the town
That his son's running out of his money,
But he's what the hell
And golfed the best china tea set
Out the back door to the peacocks.
The milkman's empties clank their language
Across the lawn and in the dawn
The woman that does
Finds the house at sixes and sevens,
All at sea. A broken ironing board
Where someone surfed with me
Last night, all the way to America.

The Singer's House

A year in Belfast. Time enough to know
Which way the wind blows, whether north
Or south along Botanic Avenue. 'Tel-lay-o.
Tel-lay-o.' Newsboy 'tis no 'neighbourly murder'.

Cúchulainn stalked round a rosebed,
Slunk behind a dank privet.
A dull thud. A crimson riveted forehead.
Darkcrushed dawn grass where he lay.
Charlie Chaplin feet splayed heavenward.

Out of the singing house,
We have tried song.
Though the streets seemed all wrong;
The lilt and lift leave the lips.

Funerals at funerals. Moonhelmet men
Stop and circle. Hedgehogged in batons and rifles,
A perspex wagon train waits but the apaches ken
Not to circle but come over the top with milk bottles
And flailing tomahawk from a coalhouse scuttle.

Out of the singing house,
We have tried song.
Though the streets seemed all wrong;
The lilt and lift leave the lips.

High over Divis, a tin bee
Dips its white proboscis tip
Into the red-brick flower of the city.
Sunshafts at midnight slant along battlement chimneys.

The Van Gogh Letters

Dear
    Theo,
Because we do not belong
    to ourselves,
 I want the lark   to sing
the inaccessible joy
        of my own heart's theology
    a gospel
            like miners'   Sunday sunshine:
    Indeffessi favente deo.

    Theo, I've lived as I could
                —haphazardly–
            relied too much
                on your charity,
            lost time by bread.
                    But you know La Sorcière,
            the abandoned pit,
    a deep-cut
            wagon rut
                through
                    the Borinage:
        as if the landscape were whipped.
The pollard willows I have only sketched pitifully
    but soon I shall attack the cypresses and the stars
        'til my heart is just one reality of icy blue on yellow.
                    But I know
                    the black
                        crow
                        bent
                        and
                        slung
                        low
                    over the corn
        and the pack horses   on the towpaths at Laeken.

18

Theo, I am dying
                with homesickness
      for the land of pictures.
   Outside   the wind   in the trees
       writes my name,
                Vincent.

Morandi

bottle vase jar
arranged in timid faith
an altarpiece without angels
does a bottle
long for hands?
a vase
a flower?
a jug
recall the musk of wine?
braille
whispers
in a
scullery tap
silence furred in must
through time
our
thumbprints
buried under dust
morandi
in the chess of your mute
tautologies
bottle a bottle   vase a vase   jug a jug
let not the angels
forget
to pray for us

Rough Guide
for Paula Harkin

It's in the leg of Allen Pot, arse-end of nowhere;
        past the green-orange hall;
forenenst Sammy Seven Suppers' wall,
        where you'll pass a wrecked Vauxhall
in Bar-the-Dure's Lane; there should be—if he's back again—
        a light in Matha Moore's entry,
but don't take it (nor the Double-ditch nor Back-burn pad),
        veer left at Hawk-Eye's midden,
then sharp right as if you're headed for Tamlaght-Finlaggin
        and you'll see Scobbie's J.C.B. ;
go canny for there's a mad dog in the sandpit
        that belongs to Flea Magee;
then take your first turn left, as if you're making
        for the Murder Hole
road through the Windy Gap, and you'll see Cutmore's
        lorry carryin' Kelly's coal
slap-bang middle of the yard and it's himself you're after—
        he's married on the Cruscaddens
who've a satellite dish foreby a monkey puzzle tree
        in the big-end b&b on the Fivemile Road bends
and you'll swing round to the front door. But was it Sid
        or Sean Cutmore you say you know,
for, if you're askin' directions, up there they'll no ken
        their arse from their elbow.
What? Seamus Cutmore. Sure that's neither it nor the same road
        at all.
It's in the leg of Allen Pot, where the Curly meets
        the Castle Burn at the blue Orange hall.

Between

for Jennifer on rope and trapeze

Between hanged man and hawk's hover
The earth and the crow's nest,
A spider's web is woven,
A pendulum at rest.

Between a ring and rosie,
Husha—then all fall down,
Your bodies ungripped gravity
Swung round in upside down.

Between a feather and falling,
Weightless weight and lead.
You carve an angel's equipoise
Between the living and dead.

Between

*For Alfonso Monreal, who said life in Mexico was
proverbially lived entre copa y copa (between shots).*

Between El Tamborazo
And a lambeg drum;
Dom Chuy's pouring mescal,
Charlie Lavery's passing rum;
Entre copa y copa.

Between all Los Dorados
And the IRA;
Rain on mission huts,
Sun on the campanile;
Entre copa y copa.

Between Tierra Colorado
And Gallaher's Green;
Among baroque contortions,
Royal Avenue's fat queen;
Todo entre copa y copa

Cuenta el aparacedio?
Or *How's about man?*
Was in tacos el rapido
Or a street chip van?
Entre copa y copa.

Between all Los Plateros
And the watchtowers on Cavehill;
The shot within the broken glass,
Old men on window sills;
Entre copa y copa.

Between a silent corner
And a fiddle in the bar,
Would a rooster know
When the cows came home
Or a hearse from a wedding car?
Todo entre copa y copa.

23

The Ballad of Hella Olsen

'I have heard the mermaids singing'—T.S.Eliot

From Belfast to Copenhagen
From dockyards ships weave seas
Hear my heart on an Irish morning
Hammer a songship for thee.

See how she slips into morning
Crashing green through the bay
An aiker threading the water
Trawling a song from the spray.

Flying fish in the forenoon
Skimming a dance in her wake
And a selkie leapt into the evening
All for merriment's sake.

But you say the song is a keening
Salt in the North-Sea spray
A wind whipping dull grey water
Through Copenhagen Bay.

Ah, come down from the black-rocked harbour
Bronze mermaid of the quay
From the ropes and chains and netting
I sing this song for thee.

And I'm singing for ever and ever
Through a wind night's cold North Sea
'Til waters are ringed in our laughter
And the mermaids are singing with me.

Belfast Jazz

Sing sad city   those who stare out
                            of late-evening windows
Sing town turn red   in last sunlight lilt
Sing Stanley drunk   raggle-taggle songs
                            of blue methylate spirit
Sing white-beard Mere grace notes carved from the runic
                            flute in Cornmaket
Sing Patrick, too,   snake-banishing songs
                            from the Holy-wood
Sing spinning songs   from the thread of this toenail
                            moon beaten into gold lunulae
Sing walkie-talkie   late-night soldiers
                            out among drinkers
Sing stars over-Tone   Cave Hill and the lullaby gantries
Sing Protestant grocers in east Belfast,
                            wilder country and west airs
Sing man   the fifteen to one,
                            you're the lucky one, she came in
Sing late-night taxi-men foxtrot to tango, are you working
                            right through 'til morning
                            —aye—it's all right
Sing stars high   white indifference wheel on
                            through the Aldergrove jet-line tonight
Sing rattle-roving   Larne boat-train, the humming
                            electrification of the late nightlit fairy palace
Sing Tom Waits'   tomcat throat-rattle down tin-pan
                            alley back-to-back housing again.
Sing   for the dockwind
                            Sea-Cat come home,

    While the woman leaves
          the late-evening window
    And Stanley goes home
          to no home
    And the toenail moon
          still rising

And the city like Rachel
                mourning her children
And her old white Queen's deserted
                stare down Royal Avenue
While Tom Waits' tomcat
                still plays down tin pan alley
And stars and prostitutes come out.

For William Carlos Williams

Who really gives a fuck
About the importance
Of the little red wheelbarrow,
Its wheels in muck
Or pebble-dashed by rain?
Have you not noticed,
Since Tetley's tea bags,
We'll not take time
To brew loose tea again?

For Alan on Shetland

See where a gull glides
And a child is singing,
This is your machair,
Early tide of ancient things:
A wind of gifts,
A sea of clouds,
All things of the rain's
Telling purity.
And a selkie comes out of the sea—
Breeding, shining.

Jesus

I was wild as a crow but I'd know
They were gonna nail me sometime—
For all that wreckin' around the Temple casino
Or anarchy on the sea, at Galilee,
When we broke the fishing quotas.
I knew they'd need me at most for all those
Poussins they wanted or pilot chat show hosts'
Question time programmes with *'The Holy Ghost.'*
'King of the Jewry?' Kiss my arse.
I was, am and will always be
A regular three-to-one revolutionary.
And I know he knows that I know
He's gonna make a name for himself,
By leaving me high and dry on the shelf,
When he sings like a canary to the cops.
Foresight is just nerve facing reality:
Like the cock crowing and me knowing
They'd a crown of thorns for my locks.
But—for Christ's sake—I didn't really know
I was Christ 'til it was too late
And there were soldiers at the garden gate,
And Judas with his kiss worth tuppence,
Saying I'd got my comeuppance at last.
When it was finished and the die was cast,
I did know Golgotha's Vinegar and *Here we go*
Would keep as gospel truth after the wake,
When men remembering their youth
Spoke of heydays that were full and forever fine.
Unbelievable days, when the water was wine.

Sam Beckett's Xylophone
for Jamshid Mirfenderesky

*My uncle would ask: If it took a man a week to walk a
fortnight, how long would it take to sandpaper an elephant
into a greyhound?*

    wherein-when?
    what-abouts?

    whither-why-ward?
    whence-abouts?

    was-will-ever?
    was-will-never?

    what-abouts?

    whither-ward?
    why-abouts?
    what-will-ever?
    will-would-never?

    what-toward?

    would-should-ever?
    would-could-ever?

    when-abouts?

    ah! could-will-man?
    wherein-whenever?
    whomsoever-will?

    whatsoever-can?

The Clock Man

*In Glasgow bars friends called him the 'Clock Man'; one arm was
shorter than the other.*

Half-tight on gin-wit the clock-man may be gone sometime
    (He's glottaled all the stops)
Propped a bar for a full month of Sundays
    (Far out in a land time forgot)
Where he's mirrored, one arm a foot short the other
    (At quarter to three or quarter past nine)
His left sure the right's making headway and by the clocks
    (Knocked back to wintertime)
He's two optics up on the meantime if ticks for talk
    (Or a quart's poured in a pint-pot)
In a happy hour, when his omega's way out of sync
    (With the town clock)
Winding up in the Wild Rover, where it's always, aye ever
    (Ever after one more)
At closing time carried out into Saturday's Sabbath
    (With a moveable feast of golden Marthober),
He'll sing like a cuckoo for little red robin or summer spent in Siam
    (In bars that are full as the Lord)
Keeping time to a tune with a moon full of rainbows
    (And detached from the earth's umbilical chord).

The Connoisseur

He orders horsemeat, does not
Hedge his bets: Nijinsky; L'Escargot;
Shergar; Red Alligator, rare; Red Rum;
Thoroughbreds trained by Sir Alex Ferguson.

He orders dogs by form on the inside track:
From Crufts to Jack Russells bred way back;
Corgies (free-range or by appointment to the Queen);
Greyhound starters, steak from the five-fifteen.

He orders drinks from the guide to good lemonade:
A 7-Up (1963); oak-aged Coke; Vintage Orangeade;
Cantrell & Cochrane decanted at room temperature;
And pop from the cellars and fine yards of *Alka-Seltzer*.

Northlight
for Jimmy Hughes, photographer

Nowhere but north,
    where tin-light bridled folk
Yoked man and beast
    and left the farmhouse nettled
In the rain. Where weather reports time and again
    its darkest joke in doors or faces,
Wintering in graveyard angels,
    carving snow-steps in the docks.
Then *Hey*, my freckle boyface, *easy on*
    the clocks and goldilocks roll on
and fairground fair's dealing
    frost soon enough—'til the tree is
Beautifully blasted. *Easy on,*
    The child-ghost in the winding sheet
Becomes tomorrows Lammas' trader soon enough
    with Woodbine in his teeth;
For if nothing's lost then nothing's lasted
    and the image always recast:
Of Jesus men climbing hills,
    of Gethsemane souvenirs;
May well walk back down the years
    into the photograph
Or forwards into the past. Weathering well,
    a rock or salt surviving tree
Becomes the basalt's lightning, constantly
    bent into a blind monument
to old north-light or new weather.

Signs

For Ulster signs, God and discriminating tourists trust
The Guidebook: *From the Sublime to the Ridiculous*

Which lists festivals and clears up right away
Differences between Sunday (Bloody) and Friday (Good).

And it's peculiarly fine on signs, in streets or shops,
With strange languages without commas or full stops:

In signs such as

Community		The War Is
Alert	or	Over
Area		Here

Falling		Reductions Inside
Rocks	or	Kerr's Trousers
Beware		Down

There are differences in the small print between
slowing the car and starting a war
Just as there are between landslides and bargains
Offered by men with their trousers down.
These differences, though, may not be profound.

Window Gazer

Inner émigré—Seamus Heaney

Window gazer, double glazed in squall and sun
Her trees and fleeing face go round the glass aquarium.
She rubs cat comfort on the glass, breaks off a rhythm
That she taps on every second tile along the sill,
The postman past the day unfolds no gift
Except a gusty tree trespassed by wind.
Her vacant, locked, unfocused face
Stares past me, holds maddest heart in her museum;
The window is a safe and the same
Willow trees are locked on her plates.
Her high-walled garden's growing green
By another's envy 'til what seems is, is all
She might have been – is not:
She meets herself in mirrors down the hall
And starts from strange abstractions;
Finds that all possessions art has made
Her émigré in the uncrossed ways of the heart.

Blue	Road	Dark	Soul
Blue	Road	Dark	Soul
Time	Buries	Every	Agreement
Like	Thumbprints	Under	Dust
Love	Like	Lust	Leaves
Little	But	Regret	Solicitors
Letters	A	Locket	Of
Hair	Curled	In	Velvet

Thanks a Million

I'd truly like to thank you:
for the poems without metaphors;
and the handles without doors;
for the shoes without a lace;
and the stars without a space;
for the armies with no captain;
and shrinks who were insane;
for perfume that was poison;
and the summers full of rain;
for mornings that were evenings
and the planes without a wing.
Yes. I'd like to really thank you
for the choir that couldn't sing.

Sooner Than Return

Deirdre, in old Irish mythology, is the gold albino
that would eat spokes out of the wheel—Padraic Fiacc

sooner	put my prick in a flymo
sooner	shave with a cheese-grater
sooner	shite a brick
sooner	navigate with a Braille compass
sooner	turn tricks in the cemetery
sooner	use nettles as ointment
sooner	love Judas
sooner	marry an executioner
sooner	meditate on a power drill
sooner	talk to a deaf perfectionist
sooner	seek warmth in an abbatoir
sooner	carve sand or mist
sooner	enlist, ride with Fergus in his car

than return or take Deirdre's hand.

Call Me Henri

Call me *Henri*,
I will walk with you
In The Tuilleries
Drink coffee
By a vase
Or spend an hour
Near palaces
Where Kings
Lie in long grass,
Absolved, forgotten,
By history.
I will pass
The courts
Of silent justice

Call me *Henri*,
I will call you
Eve or *Anaïs*.
As you balance
une pomme
in each hand.
When you got lost
I looked for you
Among roses and
geometric beds.
I was looking
For justice and love
Among the old,
And newly-weds.

Old Lover

Talk to me in the Café Poirot,
Legs akimbo on the settee
'Til a summer's easy fluency
Worn lightly as your reddest dress
Dispels old analytic histories
Written by women, sentences
Scored in my body, terminology,
Definitions missing me.
Like Jonah, I fell asleep at sea
In promises I could not keep
For I'd already lost the chart
Of what was or is or was meant to be
When you altered the room's geometry
Saying simply *Leave with me*.
I did, just when I thought I'd hid
My body in a monk's garb of flirtation,
Murdering sensuality.

So talk to me in the Café Poirot
Among the white cups and faces
In the moments between the spaces
In the spaces between the moments,
You know you know how
I will think of you then and now.

Walking to Autumn

Walking to autumn south through Honshu
cement dust on leaves, cold fat carp in the ryokan

Can you eat rice for breakfast?—I can—can you?
the sea's getting colder in these warmer latitudes—

Still walking to autumn south through Honshu
—and the clopidy-click-ity, clickity-clop of looms—

Weaving kimonos in the shops of the old capital
gaijin on a journey—still—gaijin at its end—

Walking to autumn south through Honshu
—with dragonflies dying in the heart—

heads of uncut rice too—south— across Ishikari River
—on through Sapporo—

Cold Winter Olympic Stadium—a concrete dam,
a car cemetery in the rain—ah! fuck Japan—

The oil lamp's shiver in August, the sea colder too
—Russian seal traders from Sakhalin—

Navetsa cement factory; rain; no haiku
—lighting cigarettes under a railway bridge—no—

How do you do? Cold Sapporo. Deserted
Winter Olympic Stadium—car cemetery in rain—shops shut—

Still, walking to autumn on through Honshu
—the diesel truck driver shouting—

Gaijin in a mirror, the gold rice harvest uncut
but—still—walking to autumn south through Honshu—

Cold, fat carp in the ryokan. Can you eat rice for breakfast?
I can—can you? Walking to autumn south through Honshu.

Birds

for Claire Carpenter, painter and printmaker

I can't pretend I could make head nor tail of it—
The lesser-spotted love song of the long-tailed tit.
Nor could I decipher its different decibel
From a thrush that threw a warbler or a nightingale's knell.
A painter who argued a white crow dark
Tippexed sparrows, like commas, out into the snow
And herons just settled as brief question marks
Migrated from China to some place I don't know.
A poet who killed two birds with one stone,
Brought blackbirds in flight out of mere printer's pie
And a bird in his hand, just adapting in dye,
Started breeding as two in the bush of the poem.
A poet's painting the black crow white 'til it flies
    as no crow flies.
A painter's two stones evolve as one bird
    in an orlithological guise.

As The Crow Flies

Never
    Be
    Mechanical.
        Always intuit.
        Live in
           the depths
               where light
                    is
                    precious.
                        If
                    you're gonna
                    fly.
              Fly
          with
        the crow
      that
    doesn't fly
    as the
crow flies.

The Road to La Oliva
two roads diverged—Robert Frost

I know there's a lovely road from Ixopo into the hills,
African hills with names like a blessing.
And lovely beyond all singing of them, lovelier still
When I walked that way with Lessing.

I know there's a lovely road past a Monaghan shed,
Past dolmens and the ancient dead to where the *wheep*
And *snick* of a fisherman's reel cut clear across the lough,
As Kavanagh might have said.

I know too of a lovely road through stunted Scots pine
Up the sides of a Faroese valley and when it's fine
The bee-buzz and salmon leap are heard in fresh cut hay.
Or so I've heard Knut say.

And a lovely road where the Wakonda-Auga snakes
And splices its tin-light in tributaries, before it breaks
Out of Indian territories full of cactus and stone.
I've heard its lonesome whistle, heard it sung from Kesey
        or Cohen.

And a lovely road through Albufeira's almond trees,
Where a white-haired wind shakes petals into the breeze
Bringing them down like perfume and snow,
In a wind you'd guess that Lorca might know.

Aye, and a lovely road, from Chang Mai beyond the Ping;
Fringed with citronella, jasmine and hidden cicadas who sing
From the verges of rubber plantations, out of the sunlight,
A road taken once by Kenny White.

  Aye, and there's the road for La Oliva:
  The road where cactus grows in gardens.
  The road where black dogs say beware.
  The road where winds don't ask for pardon,

Where red soil stains your face, your hair.
The road where the olive is bitter;
Where stones break down at night.
Should you take that road you'll be bitter and broken
And you'll travel alone and light.

Shore Road, Donegal

Before the storm,
invent starlings
ceasing to sing

in hesitant
silence
like fog thickening;

before thunder,
hear plank
after plank

drop from clouds
stacked low or likely
in pewter banks.

What hits the bog road
hard is neither here nor there,
but stare or say it's hailstones

even as they melt
in sunshowers
or pelt

the yard and leave it
rinsed and settled,
momentarily tarred in tin.

Silver yarn as power lines,
briefly etches itself in
from farm to farm

as rivets settle
in puddles
weeping solder in the road

from farm to farm
down to a scythe
of bay.

Momentarily,
a sea-full of metal fillings
glints blindingly

before swift har
draws in quickly
to disperse metaphors

and birds on a foreshore
sandbar.
What stays stationary

long enough to say
where far grey-dark sand
or dark-grey sea

meet
indistinguishably
beyond watercolour or word,

when known boundaries
melt? All that remains
is an ink-ling to invent

or replace the road
where it was, or may,
or might have been, or bent

or may be still,
before pier or kirk
disappear leaving

language going on
like a windscreen wiper
driving into the mirk.

12 July

Flutes for magpies, whistling whin
brimming in the farm lanes'
yellow heat;

Blanket on the Ground;
splayed feet in a two-mile
tramp to the town.

Houl me up 'fore I fall,
jap me brains 'gin a wall
says the Bar-the-Dure,

Keep Kick-the-Pope for town.
The night before they'd gathered in
from Edenmore and Ballyquin

And threw dice
into a tin
for the donkey Mary.

Purple and flute-poised
Billy's boys lost in the noise
of Derry defended again.

We will not recant
the minister says in the field
we're proud people and will not yield

And Ciaran McGrotty,
the only Catholic drunk in town
says wryly

he's fed up looking at Protestants.
Jimmy. Cog-oxtered Jimmy
Cane—not O'Kane—

With a whole day's drink
in his head will waken
the wain or 300 years dead

And Willie. *How's about you?*
Have you left the black preceptry car
parked half-mast, ticking over

Outside the Crown Bar
and Liquor Saloon?
All day drunk, deaddrunk

Deaddrunk, deaddrunk,
Hit the rum-bottle drum
Or the 5-glass Teacher's

While traders, whores, preachers
follow, followed the raggle-taggle
order to the field.

We are a proud people.
Not an inch will we yield.
We are primary paint

Poured straight from the tube,
Sprint up an entry
After a lock'a lube

And a staggering man
with a red hand who's done
what he could.

Ballymena Burial

A rain held day.
He talks fresh hope
Over another new dead.
The organ stops playing
Pre-recorded music.
Later his hand
Will command
Fallen clay.

Cars broke journeys.
As the coffin moved shakily
Into the street,
Low clouds pass over Slemish.
Patrick's sheep ... White sheep,
White sheep. When it is
Finished ... each will turn
to his own way.

A litany drifts down-
Wind and away
Over tombs to where
The pregnant granddaughter
Waits white-faced by the cars.
In the clay's falling arc,
His laboured voice
Breaks, *Tilly* ...

My wee critter ... Tilly.
He calls through a dark doorway.
If she'd asked he'd buy
her trinkets again from Saturday fairs
But have little to say of love.
He leaves the cemetery, hung
On a drizzled raincoat.

It will inherit space among
Weightless wire hangers.
He will stare suspiciously,
When the nurse like a thief
Moves quietly clearing her things away,
And invent in vacancy or grief
A solicitor brother who he'll *put wise to them*.

Trees on wavering walls
In darkening rooms,
Heavy with ointment and absence.
Long grey afternoons
Slant in shadows of morphia.
He wanders through her time of better weathers
'Til beyond rains, he's on green hills faraway.

One day,
When the wind blows,
He will stand still.

A cortège turns into the cemetery.
A slow queue turning in mizzle
Towards a point in eternity
Where earth is heaped red.
Rain, barely, fly-flecking cheeks.
The order of marble
In the house of the dead.

And a stone angel
Stares through the gates.

Hobbo
for Medbh McGuckian

As I am hobbo, so you are the last fine wine
Of my red-weather days.
When a town turning summery slips by,
Almost drunk, at a carriage's window,
My shadow falls past your doorway,
And on to where the hedge-high light's
Weaving tapestries into the hawthorn's silence.
I live between summer's spittle in egg-bush
And the mood of sparrows building nests.
Though bed is my cardboard unfolded,
And my beer and cheap wine days end
In the thin unwashed smell of a hay-ending summer,
Accept, I lay me to rest in a railway siding,
Accept, what comes here
But moons among garbage, bright spiral bones
Of bedsprings, planks ripped off roofs, beer cans,
And tumbledowns. How beautifully high
Now nettles trellis nerves on a low-slung moon –
a rat's feet makes tremble – as light breaks
All my dark houses into identities:
Here—where the Victorians cast iron for me:
To make Mondrians of the moon.

Old Scores

I

Until a landscape is named it does not exist.

—Magnus Magnusson

BBC live coverage of the World Cup.
Denmark 0, England 3.
We'd reached the quarter-finals, after '53, repeatedly.
Pan: Trafalgar Square going mental.
Commentary: it's monumental.

RTE late highlights of the World Cup.
Denmark 0, England 3.
Their first semi-final since '66, the Moore years.
Close up: Pat Staunton's studio suit.
Commentary: Brazil, next game, will end in tears.

The Viking airwaves were silent.
Their attacks offside on BBC and RTE.
Nobody's ball was signed by Gunnar Solskaer.
Nobody was making Danish pastry.

II

I've a question to ask
All my old Protestant friends:
How do you spell Cam-o-gee?

The prize is a week's soccer
Tour with Man City in Buncrana,
Or half-time in Tir-na-og with a cup of tea.

Fly Fishing

... every fly-tie and pool has a name—Lawrence McIlroy

     Bog-fly. Cock-robin. Sooty-olive.
             Teal-blue silver.
                  The Bull's Hole's flooded.
There's a freak fresh in the river.

     Silver-doctor. Dark Rosaleen.
             Napper Tandy or Dunkeld.
                  The Lamb's and Bull's Hole's flooded.
The Meeting's and The Innler meld.

     Alexander Greenwell's Glory.
         Tie her up.
             We're on our way:
Snatcher Lou's on the river; it's pishing trout all day.

In Memoriam, Uncle Bill & Granny Bond

Uncle, I've been in driftwood spaces,
Far from warmed pyjamas at the range.
The west witchcraft and a light that's strange,
Falling over Looney's land and Clare.
Here could, should and would
Become I can, I will and dare,
I climb the outhouse stair
—as curlew dawn swings anglepoised
in the breaking light's direction—
To make pictures in bone and stone
And all that's flotsam fit for resurrection
In this tidal, stone-built, kingdom.

Evening's holding off, putting on,
The light 'til it falls low, slow and replete
Down Milltown Malbay's street
Where I listen still for your steel-tipped feet
Between a mangle and scullery outhouse.
Sometimes, when I'd go through, she'd say—
He's out there tinkerin', futerin' away
At something below a skylight
And I'd go through to find you
Among holstered awls, turps,
Nails in biscuit tins,
And gold curled shavings by the bin:
A life hit flush by love.

Uncle, send me a voice,
With the spirit level,
While that ole devil called love
Plays smooch long-wave
On the wireless.

If it can't be used in seven years
Then throw it out, she said,

So you'd put it by in the shed,
Like a poet stores a fallen word's
Desuetude
In the brain's backyard,
'Til new dynamic usage makeshifts time again
Gives elbow room
To driftwood or forgotten word.
A bicycle clip, a swatch of leather.
This, this; that, that:
Until spring-loaded together,
A latch for the door appears.
And a metaphor's perfected.

Cúchulainn Unbound

I
The Burial of the Dead

St. Patrick's is the kindliest day,
Breeding lilies in Milltown cemetery,
Mixing memories of Carson and Connolly.
Between shoures sote and tiocfaidh ár lá
The roofs of Belfast and river glar
Rinsed in wet glitter, blue bottle shiney again.
The twelfth of July surprised me:
The helicopters flown from Divis and Cave Hill;
The Garvaghy Road empty, eerily still,
Where once orangeboys and newsmen were hemmed in
Between residents' groups and the RUC.
And when we were children, painting kerbs
Or spraying murals on the Lower Falls,
Staying at my Uncle Archibald's (oul' elephantiasis memory)
On the green hills near the Bogside, outwith city walls
She took me out on a bin-liner bobsleigh:
She said *Johnny! Fuck's sake, Johnny!*
Hold on tight. And down we went singing reggae
Ev-e-ry little thin' gonna' be aw-right.
Our bobsleigh signature, a brief history, lay buried in the snow.
I nattered 'til late in the night, going south in summer
(Leaving the north knee-deep in political bullshite),
Double-locked the car and, in the preoccupied 26 counties,
Drank, blew loads in Temple Bar.

What are these smouldering stumps?
Dismembered dolls, smashed TV sets and tyres,
Red marigold gloves and kneecapped tables dumped
In wasteground pyres amidst the red-brick terraces?
Son of man, it's time to say or guess
For this heap of broken images, gift-wrapped in ticker tape
And spliced with cricket scores, became the Ulster mess
As Big Ben tolled the hours.

Is there relief or redress for an ulcerous history
As perpetual rain pours off Cave Hill?
None. The only shelter's under MacArt's fort,
(Come in under the shelter of MacArt's fort)
And listen! Tone's voice above the M2's hum and linen mills.
Oh, my dear, green, fucked up, godforsaken place.
How can I embrace thee?
The summer soldiers gone;
The sybil left to ruminate: *Stay me with apples,*
Comfort me with flagons. My love. I'm sick of hate.

> *Snowdrops and daffodils.*
> *Song in the night.*
> *Wedding bells. Wishing wells.*
> *Say it's all right.*

We gave her roses years ago; we called her rose of Doire.
Yet when she came back late to the oak grove
—flashbulbs on her Eurovision car—
Mein Irish kind, my eyes did not fail:
I was living in a council estate,
In Derry beyond the pale;
The rose garden was kept locked;
Ball Games Prohibited;
We wanted roses and chocolates,
Not tracts by the bed or the priests
Climbing again to the altars of Baal.
Il y a un jardin Espagnol, un jardin Italien;
Ily y a un jardin de trefles et, bein sur, de rouges main;
Je ne vous ai jamais promis un jardin de roses.

Mandy Mo, famous clairvoyant, politico,
Has a bad cold, but none the less,
Watches Easter snow fall from a window
In Stormont and knows the Unionist card
Ulster Says No is finally finito, a must-go area.
In the room Seamus and David come and go.
The room just might be bugged so Gerry's talking low.
These she said are your cards. The Magician.

Houdini of the maze, who picks locks, shapes
Paintbrush or armalite into a ballot box.
Here is the Prima Donna. The Lord of Situations,
Rabble-rouser of the docks.
Here is the one-eyed merchant. Here the wheel.
But who's afraid of Harland & Wolff,
When the steel's shipped in and drillers are playing golf
Or signing on? The Phoenician in Sailortown sails round
In an automobile. Here's the hanged man.
Fear death by ennui, rebirth by a fry or the blood of the lamb.
This card's a Pearl Insurance Life Policy.
Thank you. If you see dear Mr. P.
Tell him I'll bring the horoscope, myself.
I'm sure it's still f. the pope
So it's hardly necessary.
One can be less careful these days?

Unreal city, after the burning of Lundy
A crowd flowed over the bridge at Sandy Row.
I had not thought death had undone so many.
And in the Ancient Antediluvian Order of the Buffalo
They priced Kerr's Pinks and a pint.
Phantoms. Horse spancels, harness, plumes, flutes
And ancient swords of war flowed
Over the hill, behind a black car, into Glengall Street,
All keeping time with sackbut, dulcimer and lute,
And there I saw one I knew and cried, 'Bowler!
You who landed with ships on Gideon's Green,
Have you seen her whose song is the dove
Step into the banqueting house under the banner of love?
Or has she disappeared?'
Those corpses planted year on year!
O keep the dog far hence that's friend to men
Or with his claws he'll dig the corpses up again.

II
A Game of Chess

    The seats laqueria of beads,

From Afric via Billy Seeds & Sons,
Car Accessories.
The Mazda Cosmo dials
Glowing amber in the dark,
The needle climbing 90
As we gathered speed
Past mossy bawn
And topiaried demesne,
Out on the open road,
Where Geraldis Cambrensis
Saw the spotted toad
And prophesied the Gael in chains.
Wrong turn. Border-map quirk.
Unapproved road sign:
SNIPER AT WORK.
Reverse. Start again.

What was the chair she sat in?
    The chair she sat in was leatherex;
    set before the VDU (wired with electric flex);
    wherein, the great book of 'classified' lists:
    the names and photo-fits of terrorists.

And to whom shall atonement be made?
    To the Almighty, strong as a constant searchlight,
    so that the city hath no need of moon at night;
    to one that knoweth all who sing and lament,
    having judgement of incidents, listening alone
    to the supergrass on the confidential telephone.

And who shall stand over the sacred gate?
    The sentry of surveillance, he shall stand over against the gates
    to command them to be lifted, early or late,
    for the unmarked car of the Secretary of State at four
    or 'that bastard lifted in the wee small hours' the night before.
    He shall stand at the gate.

What then of the cell within the gate?
    The cell shall be, with iron bed, secure,

a rough thin blanket; a slatted steel door.
The smell of Vim or urine on the floor.

How wilt the hours then pass within the cell?
The hours thou dwelleth there, not well but long,
thou wilt remember well, confess thy wrong.
When thy confessor come to thee therein,
Then shalt thou say, *Forgive me, Father,*
I have sinned. He shall direct thee then
to closed or open doors and tell thee sinner:
Go and sin no more.

> *My nerves are bad tonight. Twitchy.*
> *Nothing's right. Bloody bonkers army.*
> *Who's the enemy? What's the natives thinking?*
> *Dave? Still there, mite? Chrissakes. Tread lightly.*
> *Cut the walkie-talkie cackle. You wha? Awe-right?*
> I never really know what you are thinking.
> Out here alone. I think we have been in rats' alley
> Where the dead dog buries the bone.

This is the news from ITN.
Two men shot dead in Crossmaglen.
Check. Checkmate. Checkpoint.
Point-blank. Border checkpoint.
Bordering worm madness. Classified check.
Ireland's Shatterday Night:
Broighter & Gold Albion 1   Medussa's Raft 10

Has the famine ship cleared the bay?

I shot one. I shot two. I shot thirteen more than you.
Birmingham 6. Gibraltar 4.
Focherd? Brighton? How many more?
What's that noise? The wind under the door.
With a knick knack Paddy-whack gae the dog a bone.
How many Fenians didnae gae home?
Nothing again.
Nothing.

Do you know nothing?

Pol-lice. Pull over please. Dim the lights.
Name, sir? Your passenger? Car registration?
Your licence? L or R? Everythin-awe-right?
You're late the night?
Flashlit moustache. Driving licence.
Question. Statement. Interrogation.

For Shauny-John and that's my name, a hyphenated nation,
And heaven, sir—that's p.l.c.—and that's my destination.
My DNA's pure porcellanite; my torchlit eyes are pearls;
I've crossed the border cross-dressed, a bit like Shakespeare's girls.
This borrowed van—'tis Caliban's— it's beauty is still hot.
My dinner's on the table, sir—now do you want me shot?
I'm only cartin' quarry stone, somebody nicked the trees
And this isle's yours—'tis surely yours—thou takest it from me.

Since Cullen got out the Kesh, I said so I did,
He's a header. No the full shillin'. He'd fight to fight
In an empty house. He's full of mad dog's shite.
DRINK UP. GET OUT. Emer, you keep your fling
With Ferdy hid six feet under lino like his armalites.
Gallaher's Green? A light? No problem. Aye. All right?
On Bushmills, she says so she does, he's a real wee gobshite.
Comin' in at night, strip-searchin' cupboards for messages,
Murdering fries, hacksawing the fingers off sausages—
And dirty dishes or bullworker, Deidre, left at his arse, no lie.
Anyway, I says I likes her new tricolour hair—
DRINK THE FUCK UP, GIRLS, GET OUT'A HERE—
But Cullen asks if she'd it done with a knife and fork
And what side of the kerbstones the barber worked from?
Cullen she'd tell't him, I'm sick of the same slabberin' night
After night and your action man fights.
Deidre, he's aye pantin', pawin', wanting it doggy style;
I'm not just, she tell't him, some bitch on heat.
It's me doin' time, she says. DRINK UP.
I asked the watchman in the street after him whom I sought
Whose love was finer than wine. I found him not.

TIME FOLKS. DRIVE SAFE. MIND THE COPS.
Night Tony. Night Billy, Bertie. Goodnight Gerry, David, John.
Night Emer. Cheers. Sliante. Take care.

Watchman.   When doors are tightly shut at night,
              Whose hand in shadow writes upon the walls?
2.00 am: Graffiti, graffitas, graffito;
              Declining school. Ulster Says No.
3.00 am: Graffito, graffitas, graffitorum;
              Up the IRA. The spraycan's fax and forum.
4.00 am: Graffitorum, graffitas, graffito:
              City Hall directive: use abstraction: employ Rothko.
9.00 am: Grave inscription: We Kill Touts. Malice aforesight,
              Without comparison. Mene, Mene, Tekel Upharsin.
Watchman.   When the city is silent under amber lights,
              Do men sleep with swords because of fear in the night?

III
River Baptism

Sunlit leaves on the Ormeau, return to the river's chrism.
And a voice on the bridge, through the leaves, calls:
Remember Protestantism. A red hand in the fire.
Cramner? Latimer? Ridley? But the B.A. flight climbs higher
And they're nursing Guinness to New York or Sidney.
Sky. White diary: forgotten butterfly days on the Putamayo River.
Where is my Andalusian Rose? My Shulamite's song of songs?
The journalists have gone; the Europa doorman looks lonely.
Has the famine ship cleared the bay?
Sweet Lagan run on softly 'til I end my song,
Sweet Lagan's lullaby: the Gaels have gone
And their loitering heirs, the Irish Society, Guildhall, Derry,
Londonderry, are debating correct addresses,
When at my back, two chariot wheels I hear;
To Focherd Ford, two foster brothers drawing near.

River, river, brown as beer, white combing the weir;
Making the moon fragmentary. A wolfhound in the shallows.
Paws upraised, divining, nosing, danger:

63

None. Only a water rat in the rhubarb leaves.
The dog swims the Roe at Limavady.
River, river at Pettigo, rising full of snow
Falling in Fermanagh, Antrim, Tyrone, Cavan,
Monaghan, Donegal, Sligo:
Obliterating small red clots of rowan, unmapping the border.
Moonriver and estuary—rising still—not wider than a mile:
I'm crossing you in style, today.
Bends dexter or sinister? A fresh wind blowing at last:
East-north-east: 32 millibars, rising; Malin to Finnisterre;
Weather forecast: middlin' to fair.
But at my back: the hollow laughter of an unemployed docker;
A chuckle or smile that's a coffin's brass knocker.

Surreal city,
Steal girders scaffolding the moon
The Fir Bolga building on Laganside
And in the new glass dining-rooms
Mr. Chada (www. website belshite.co.uk)
Former Indian restauranteur,
Who once served poppadums
Within earshot of orange drums,
Glides across the floor in sartorial black,
Carrying two perfectly poached eggs
(half-baptised, yoke still intact):
Your Irish Fry, Madame;
Enjoy your stay; enjoy the crack.

Abenstunden. Light changes guard.
Pigeons uncarved from Imperial architecture.
The old Queen—she cleaned up bootiful,
but is she old or true?—
Stares stonily at Res Publica down Royal Avenue
Attended by her last liegeman, Fred Temple,
Marquis of Dufferin,
Who inspects the last 'Bomb Damage Sale'
While Ulsterbuses are hailed for Ballygomartin,
Delhi Street, Candahar and Donegal Pass:

Imperial Streets within a two-mile compass.
And I, Cullen in the Red Devils' Bar
At the violet hour, fail to turn home for tea
Seeking serendipity in another pint.
I, Cullen, who took poison in the porch of my ear
And in this shameful struggle, carried away on fear,
Wrecked the lives of Emer and my son,
Saw the land go to pieces and did take up a gun,
Living from a suitcase with the brigade
In unsafe houses, constantly on the run.
I, too, have awaited the unexpected guest—
The UVF, the RA or pigs in bulletproof vests
Dinging down the door on a dawn raid.
And I have seen my son's laugh fade
In photographs curling on the prison wall,
And after closing time, I'll be turning in,
My face in the Red Devils sick of sin,
A beaten dog returning to its vomit;
Staggering home up the Lower Falls
To the stairs and unlit hall,
To Emer on whom I cannot bestow even a patronising kiss;
To Emer who turns her back on all the years we missed
And falls asleep leaving me looking for comfort
In the abyss.

Emer turns her back, meets her shadow in glass,
Recalls nights getting pissed in Donegal Pass,
(Knickers down surveillance up their ass);
For Cullen, the sleepless nightmares never end.
He wakes at dawn. He cries. He dreams again.
He dreams he's killed his son, his fiend a friend.

    Morning swims into a bar mirror in the docks.
    Emer applies a lipstick O,
    For the few customers she doesn't know.
    Mostly though it's early regulars, sipping slowly,
        getting blocked.
    And she has known them all already, known them all:

Hard-voiced men from the Shankill and Lower Falls;
And she has known them all already, known them all;
Alex gone west with a snooker cue, Georgie left with a ball.
And in the barlight, her arms with bracelets, white and bare,
And a drunk docker singing The Granemore Hare.

Has the Sea Cat docked in the bay?

O'Neill and Lizzie by the sea:
K-I-S-S-I-N-G.
First comes love, then a barrage;
The dead are taken in a horse and carriage.
Lillibulero Bullen a la.

O'Neill and Lizzie, Greenwich Reach:
Court etiquette, rudest speech.
Come O'Neill now swear to me
The Spanish ships are not at sea.
Lillebulero Bullen a la.

My Queen, he plights upon a ring
As wild geese sing or cold winds blow:
I have nothing more to give thee:
Je ne vous ai jamais promise un jardin de rose.

River Roe. Magilligan Strand.
Limavady bore me. In Derry and Raphoe
The Bishop undid me. In Belfast's Aftonland,
I kept my head low.

My feet in the Mater Memorial. My heart
In the Royal Victoria. After the incident,
The knee surgeon wept. He promised a new start.
I made no comment. What should I resent?

On Portrush Beach I disconnected the mobile phone.
Out of reach, alone; the Promenade by the sea.
Abandoned fish-and chip-wrappers in Arcady.
My humble people who expect nothing. A sales rep. Alone
In a seaside B&B. Fancy Lanzarote later in the year? Absolutely.
Fan-bloody-daby-dosy. Saw it once on satellite TV.

Father Joachim saw fire coming out of the earth:
The island's difficult volcanic rebirth;
Thunder's DATTA! DAYADHVAM!
He gave; he sympathised—then—DAMYATA—tried control;
We'd had enough of that, mon frère:
So pogue ma hone. You kiss my hole.

To Belfast then I came.
The Ulsterbuses burning;
Burning, burning, burning:
My fair Lundy.

To Belfast then I came,
Where Lagan streams were sweet;
Slept to the noise of running water:
The river to be crossed, however deep.

Deep and wide; deep and wide;
The Lagan's flowing deep and wide;
Plunge right in, lose your sin;
End up in the looney bin—
Or sing and dance at Lughnasa.

IV
Born Again

For Phlebas the Phoenician—it's all go navigation!
Across religion's -ism, across the –ish of nation;
His own Ardens Sed Virens: trading with all races;
Hoist mainsail! Set the compass! Cross exacting places!

Now, it's all go cross community grants,
It's all go two traditions,
We're playing the Sash on the Eulieean Pipes
And to hell with the tin-hut missions.

It's all go The Hilton Hotel,
It's all go Waterfront Hall;
We're pedalling dope on the Golden Mile
And the bomber's pimping a moll.

And it's all go British Telecom,
It's all go Tour Busaurus;
The pound and euro are both taken here—
So you don't need a bloody thesaurus.

Now it's all go, amazing grace,
God is both Queen and a Celtic Tiger!
But mon frère Phlebas, I hope you don't mind
When I'm broke if I borrow a fiver.

V
New Light

After the torchlight red on the sweaty faces,
The baseball bats, the graves in the hidden places,
After the unmarked car in the side street
Ticking over and the half-hearted flags
Fraying in fields of Friesians and clover.
Was it here he was fingered, done over?
After the agony of stony places
A foot patrol walking backwards forwards into Candahar
Street and plain clothes men clocking the Hatfield Bar
And the Holy Land going up in Holy Smoke with fire—
Is there spring thunder or a Medici sky in the gantries?

He who was living is now dead.
A 'candid tea-time bullet'?
Blood, fear and loathing,
But whatever you say, say nothing;
Whatever you say, say nothing.
Forensic will test the clothing.

Here there is no speech. Only silence.
Silence and the unmarked graves;
The road winding into the mountains,
And a noble shepherd writing Dantesque staves.
A woodkerne escaped from the massacre?
Drip. Drop. Drip, drop. Drop. Drop. Drop. Drop.
The man who was a capital X

In the bomb blast ended completely
                In a full stop. Somebody tidied his bits
                        And pieces into a bin.
                                Like slops.
We soon forgot.

What's that sound high in the air?
Murmur of maternal lamentation.
And about my ears a thousand helicopter blades
Clearing the Divis Flats and palisades
In South Armagh.
Falling towers.
Jerusalem Street; Adelaide.
Calvin Street; St. Jude's Parade.
On Rosepark Street and Erinvale,
The light falls veiled behind the Black Mountain.
Violet security lights on the Crumlin Road Gaol ...
Unreal.

And in the moonlight
The wind in the dry grass
 —sing-ing;
Over the empty chapel
in the Maze—
There was an empty chapel
in the Kesh—
The wind in the micromesh,
in the dry grass,
without a security pass—
Sing-ing.
I hear, m' laud,
the security lights have blown.
I see, my lord,
the prisoners have flown.

If there were song
And fire.
If there were fire and also song
As going gong of birdsong at Bealtaine,

Not of grasshopper days with no pleasure in them
Or dry grass singing the captivity and missing years,
But song that's required of us when the time for singing has come:
Song of the Shulamite; Song of the Children of Lir;
Song of the thrush in echoing timber that rinses and rings,
Piercing the silence of the Irish Sea;
Song without ending,
Conjoining fire and water, earth and air,
The dove in the tower and tree,
Singing into spring's bright blue nowhere:
Ah! *Comme oiseaux sur la branche*
Comme les voix dans la coeur de la nuit,
J'ai cherché ma liberté.

Who is the third that walks beside you?
She who has become the song of songs,
For whom the palace is prison and the anthem lament:
Let me hear her voice, in equipoise,
                              poured forth
                                   as ointment.
Climbing, climbing the ladder of thorns, into the rose garden,
Asking neither forgiveness nor pardon.
For her I hopscotch, skip and turn again,
Because I hope to turn again and turn to hope;
To advance a thousand visions and revisions
(without recriminations 'gainst Billy or the Pope)
Before the taking of potato bread and tea.
Because I hope to turn again, and turn from slights
To courage that is tenderness not might,
I ask the watchman of the Shulamite,
Whom my soul seeks, casting stones away,
'Til dawn breaks across the cemetery;
My wild roe on the mountains, my wild roe and my dove;
Borderless, unbound: the best of us is love.

Five Phases of the Moon
for Pamela Hunter

Not the moon but the watermelon
Fell through the High Rise Sofitel
Down to the Chae Phae River.
What luck. The thirteenth floor secretary
Made instantly a saint.

Without a moon
A night-flight.
A brief diamond mark.
A tail-light in the dark.

With tonight's full moon
Over Ardarra
Even the rabbits will breakfast late.

If the moon over Derry
Is not the moon over Donegal
Then the moon at the window
Of the Lough Foyle Ferry—
What thief will take it—
Or claim it at all?

A more than two thousand year moon in the pine
The bridge looks Romanesque through the tree.
The moon climbs higher into the night sky
Where everything is as it should be.